MOUNTAINS HAVE EARS

Speak to Them

CONQUERING FEAR, ACTIVATING YOUR AUTHORITY, AND MOVING MOUNTAINS THROUGH THE POWER OF DECREES

SANDRA CAVALLO

BRIDE AND DOVE
MINISTRIES
International

www.sandracavalloauthor.com

Unless otherwise noted, all Scripture quotations are from the King James Version of the Bible.

Scripture quotations marked Darby are from Biblegateway.com

Scripture quotations marked World English Bible are from Biblegateway.

Cover design: Maisie Grace
Editor: Kendra Langeteig
Author photos: Judah Avenue Photography

www.judahphotography.com

ISBN 978-1-66780-994-6
eBook ISBN 978-1-66780-995-3

Dedication
This book is dedicated to:

My mother, the late Sandra Smith. Thank you, Mommy, for your love and sacrifice, and for your Godly legacy. I only wish that you could be here for the debut of my first book.

My grandmother, the late Minnie Cobb, the librarian who inspired my love for books and reading. All those days of practically living in the library has birthed an author.

My incredible children Chris, Quenten, Kyra, and Kaloni. You are a source of joy and pride. May you walk in your destiny as sons and daughters of God. The best is yet to come.

The mountain movers. . . May this book inspire you to rise to new levels of authority and victory.

CONTENTS

CHAPTER 1

The Power of a Decree

"You shall decree a thing and it shall be established for you."

Job 22.28 (KJV)

NOT A SINGLE DROP of water fell from the faucet. With the water turned off we had officially hit rock bottom. Four children and an empty refrigerator meant that I had to find a job quickly. I called the agency that regulated my professional certification and was horrified to learn that they had no record of my credentials. Even though I had completed the program requirements, my supervisor had never submitted the paperwork for my final certification. The paperwork was now ten years old, and after several moves, babies, deaths, and life in general, I couldn't find it. The only hope of proving my credentials was if somehow the copies could be found. Without proof of my certification, all of my graduate study, work, and money were lost. The prospect of getting back to work in the teaching profession was looking hopeless.

Feelings of injustice washed over me as the warrior within began to rise. I was battling a well-established bureaucratic mountain fortified with layers of sticky red tape. I began praying in the spirit, taking authority, and decreeing that the paperwork would be found and that my certification would be released. I called the agency once again and asked if they could pull my file. The clerk on the phone reminded me that after ten years the file had probably been discarded. Although she agreed to look, I had a distinct feeling that she had already dismissed me. Several days later she called and said that she couldn't locate my file. She apologized for not being able to help and wished me the best.

I stared at the phone in utter disbelief. What on earth had just happened? Bewildered, I began questioning the outcome. Why hadn't God moved in this situation? Hadn't I prayed hard enough? Suddenly, I felt the Holy Spirit prompting me to take authority over this situation. So I issued a bold decree for justice based on Psalms 89:14: "Righteousness and justice are the foundation of your throne." What came out of my mouth next startled me. I began decreeing that the entire department would be shut down until they found my paperwork.

Within minutes the phone rang. It was the lady from the agency again. She said that after we hung up, she couldn't get back to work because she kept thinking about my file. She announced to her staff that all work would be shut down until my file was found. She and her team went into a basement vault where they searched and found an old file with my name on it. The file had been buried for years in a dusty old vault. I was so overwhelmed that I burst into tears.

Profound decrees can be birthed in places of utter desperation.

God had answered my request and the power of persistent decrees secured my victory over the bureaucratic mountain that had seemed insurmountable. The enemy had clearly been involved with working to steal what belonged to me. The bible says that "the thief only has one agenda: steal, kill, and destroy. But Jesus has come that we may have life and more abundantly." That document of certification opened the door for the provision and financial blessings that my family desperately needed. Not only did it shift us into a completely different economic status, it also shifted my trajectory. As I continued decreeing, things began to happen. This proved to be a major turning point in my life. The results were shocking.

No matter how long the problem or situation existed, it had to yield to the God-ordained purpose for my life. But it required me to release my faith with a bold decree. The enemy's *no* never trumps God's *yes*! What the enemy had hidden for years buried in a vault had to be released at the command of my decree. My decree had blown the door off the prison cell of my place of provision. Even dire situations can be transformed when you dare to decree. There is no circumstance that isn't subject to your decree because everything must acquiesce to the word of God.

At this point you may be wondering, what exactly is a decree?

Decrees are written commands issued by rulers having the effect of law. Decrees are so very powerful because they establish and release the order and will of God on the earth. They are also used to legislate and establish orders. The word "legislate" carries the full weight of its meaning: to enact, establish, and regulate.

In the legal system, once decrees are established the effects are legally binding. There are many types of decrees ranging from decrees of war, decrees of stipulation, marriage, divorce, and various laws of the land. God issues decrees and ordinances in his word that he expects his children to obey.

Kings also had full authority to enact anything into law by a decree. Once a king issued a decree in his kingdom it could not be revoked. In the book of Esther 1:19, King Ashasuerus issued a decree when he wanted to replace his wife Vashti. He pronounced an edict that young women would be gathered in Susa, the citadel, so that he could find a suitable replacement.

"If it please the king, let there go a royal commandment from him, and let it be written among the laws of the Persians and the Medes, that it be not altered, That Vashti come no more before king Ahasuerus; and let the king give her royal estate unto another that is better than she.

And when the king's decree which he shall make shall be published throughout all his empire, (for it is great,) all the wives shall give to their husbands honour, both to great and small."(Est 1:19-20 KJV)

The king's nobles were bound to implement the king's decree. As a result of that decree, Esther was chosen as the new queen.

There were more heinous decrees recorded in the bible, such as the decree issued by King Herodotus that ordered all babies born during the time of Jesus' birth to be killed. Decrees have the power to create life and death because "Life and death are in the power of the tongue. "(Prov. 18:21 KJV)

God has given us the power to legislate like Congress and decree like kings in the realm of the spirit. Within your mouth lies the power to reshape the landscape of your life. Get ready to release the power of your decree.

PAUSE AND REFLECT

1. How are you using the power of decrees to legislate in your kingdom area of influence?

_____

_____

_____

_____

2. How could the power of your decree change the landscape of your life?

_____

_____

_____

_____

CHAPTER 2
Designed for Dominion

"And God said, 'Let there be light,' and there was light."

Genesis 1:3 (KJV)

The Creation Mandate

THE FIRST BIBLICAL account of a decree in action is found in the book of Genesis. When God created the earth, it was void and without any form. However, as God speaks things begin to happen. God issues the very first decree when he speaks to the universe. At the sound of his voice the material world was formed. Despite the erroneous views of popular science, the world was created from the *ruach*, the breath, and the spoken word of God.

At the beginning of Genesis, we see a series of decrees that God uses to bring life and form to the universe:

"And God said, 'Let there be light,' and there was light. God saw that the light was good, and he separated the light from the darkness. God called the light 'day,' and the darkness he called 'night.' And there was evening, and there was morning—the first day. And God said, 'Let there be a vault between the waters to separate water from water.' So God made the vault and separated the water under the vault from the water above it. And it was so. God called the vault 'sky.' And there was evening, and there was morning—the second day. And God said, 'Let the water under the sky be gathered to one place, and let dry ground appear.' And it was so. God called the dry ground 'land,' and the gathered waters he called 'seas.' And God saw that it was good.'"

Then God said, 'Let the land produce vegetation: seed-bearing plants and trees on the land that bear fruit with seed in it, according to their various kinds.' And it was so." (Gen.1:11 K J V)

Don't miss this important principle of how God planned for his children to operate in delegated authority. If we examine Genesis 1, there are consistent recurring principles that are the prototypes for decrees:

Principle #1: Speak and Create.
Spoken words have the power to create life.

God steps onto the stage of the universe as a blank canvas and brings life, shape, and form where there was absolutely nothing. When God spoke, he simply said, "Let there be" and it was. Everything is created by the breath of his spoken words. He says, "Let there be," and the universe obeys his command.

We are created in the image of God. That means that we are designed to function according to the same creation code. The creation code is the privilege that God has given us to co-create with him. Co-creating allows us to speak into the earth and watch things come to pass. Within each of us lies the power to create. The latent power of the creation code is embedded in our physical and spiritual DNA. Creative power is oozing from every part of our being. We are endowed by God to procreate and have children made in our image. We can craft with our hands. Our minds offer endless possibilities for creativity and boundless imagination.

God allows us to decide what we will allow or create in our own little mini worlds. In most instances, our worlds are created by what we choose or because we have decided to let there be something. We gave our permission, agreement, or consent. The loan we agreed to, the marriage where we took a vow, the degree we earned. We let that be, and it was created according to this very principle. Never underestimate the power of the spoken word. When you speak, you are creating your world just as God spoke to create the world. We can apply the same principle of "speak and create" and expect results.

Principle # 2: The spirit world responds to your spoken decrees.

Within your mouth lies the creative power to speak miracles and subdue the enemy forces arrayed against your life. You are empowered to create and impart life or death and to release your decree. Your decrees also summon heaven to enforce the words you have spoken. Most people are oblivious to the fact that their words impact their world and the unseen realm. But the reality is that they do. While angelic hosts hasten to respond to words that align with God's word, the demonic waits with bated breath to enforce ill-spoken words. The ability to create means that decrees and words carelessly uttered from our mouths can have adverse effects and create chaos.

The universe waits to receive its commands and directives from you. Just one word is packed with enough atomic power to create a world of success or disaster. So choose your words wisely. How many times have you said something only to regret it later, but the damage was already done? It is critical that our minds and thoughts align with the heart and mind of God and are guided by the Holy Spirit.

The bible says: "Life and death are in the power of the tongue." But it doesn't stop there, it goes on to say that "they who love it will eat the fruit thereof." (Prov.18:21 KJV)

This means that a harvest is produced by the power of our words. I am always amazed by people who sow a word, behavior, or thought and expect a harvest other than what they've sown. You can't plant apple seeds and then expect a crop of oranges when it's harvest time. Words uttered as decrees become the seeds of tomorrow's life harvest. Negative confessions create crop failure, but powerful Holy Spirit-filled words spoken in season will produce a fruitful crop. Why? Because Jesus has already informed us that "Verily I say to you, that whosoever shall say to this mountain, Be thou taken away and cast into the sea, and shall not doubt in his heart, but believe that what he says takes place, whatever he shall say shall come to pass for him." (Mark 11:23 KJV) The great news is that you are included in the "whoever."

Principle # 3: Your calling power.

"And out of the ground the Lord God formed every beast of the field, and every fowl of the air; and brought them unto Adam to see what he would call them: and whatsoever Adam called every living creature, that was the name thereof." (Gen. 2:19 KJV)

When God brought the animals to Adam to name them, he was essentially saying, whatever you call them that's what they will be. This scene is about Adam's training for reigning. Naming the animals was part of the delegated authority given to Adam by God. God gave Adam authority over earth to rule and govern. Adam's job of naming the animals were decrees that established the animal kingdom on the earth. The power to reign over creation was consummated by his voice speaking words on the earth as the delegated king. God created man and he gave him the mandate to have dominion over his creation. In this first act of co-creation, God allowed Adam to test-drive his God-given authority. Adam is not just calling and randomly speaking into the earth. This authority is recognized by the animals who respond to his command.

God gives us our own territory to call the shots, coupled with the creative license to create and name books, businesses, situations—the possibilities are limitless. Nowhere is this principle of "calling it" on greater display than in the creative license that parents have to name their children. God allows us the privilege of co-creating with him. Parents exercise the power of call when they name their children. Names are decrees that have been issued and established over a person. This creative license is not just relegated to procreation.

Like Adam, your decree, once issued, establishes law, boundaries, and the purposes of God on the earth. Your world is created by what you decide to call it and what you say. God has given you the power through the spoken word to "call it." So, what are you going to call it? What are you calling your children, your finances, business, marriage, your job? What are you calling your health? What have you been calling the situations and things in your world? What are you saying? What are you legislating?

You have been designed for your dominion to be released through the power of your call. Wherever you go, wherever you find yourself, remember to be careful of your words because it becomes whatever you call it. Each of us is given authority by God to rule in our jurisdictions. Your realm includes everything God has entrusted to you. Your job, mind, will, emotions, finances, relationships, your family, business, neighborhood. However, it's impossible to establish rule without authority.

Authority is the legal power or right to command or act. If you examine the word "authority," you see that the root of this word is "author," from the Latin word *auctor*, which translates as "originate" or cause to come forth. God originates, creates, and brings into being. Because God is the author of the universe, he has all authority.

He authorizes his children to operate in his authority here on earth. To authorize means to give authority, the legal power or right to act. Authority is delegated by God, but must be given expression through sound and released by our mouths. God has given us the kingdom authority to transact business here on earth as his representatives. Everything we do becomes kingdom business. We have the delegated authority to act on his behalf. Decrees empower us to legislate as the sons and daughters of God. When we make those decrees, it is not done in and of ourselves, but in the name of Jesus.

The kingdom expression of that authority is found in your decree. What king could rule on his throne without ever issuing a verbal command? That king certainly wouldn't have a kingdom for very long. You have been designed for dominion. For too long, this revelation has been veiled and at times hidden from the church. Authority positions the child of God to take their rightful place in the earth far above all power and principalities.

Each of us has our own territory that God has given us to influence for the kingdom. The first place that we must conquer is the territory of our own life. However, before we can govern the world, we must be able to first govern ourselves. We must be able to rule our own finances, appetites, thoughts, bodies, and so on.

If we go back to original intent, Satan was never meant to be the god of this world. Instead, the world was designed to be ruled and inhabited by the children of God. You can't have dominion without a domain. You are called to dominate the domain or territory that God has delegated to you through powerful decrees. Failing to decree is forfeiting the awesome mandate to have dominion.

PAUSE AND REFLECT

1. What are you calling the things that God has given you dominion over in your mini universe?

   _____

   _____

   _____

   _____

2. What are you creating with the power of call?

   _____

   _____

   _____

   _____

CHAPTER 3
Checking Your ID

"And the evil spirit answered, "Jesus I know, and
Paul I know, but who are you?"

Acts 19:15 (KJV)

CASSANDRA AND JULIA had worked together in a bar for years. They naturally became friends when they realized that they had much in common. The women shared similar backgrounds. They had both been adopted from their home country of the Dominican Republic. Ironically, both women had been raised by single mothers. The two also looked so much alike that everyone thought they were sisters. When Madison decided to find her birth family, she took a DNA test and discovered that she and Julia really were sisters. As it turned out, they had seven more siblings. Their birth parents had put their children up for adoption because they couldn't afford to take care of them.

These sisters are like so many other people struggling to find their identity. It's human nature to want to know your true identity and birth origins. The world system is constantly pressuring us to conform to its mold, and it's all too quick to brand and label us.

Unfortunately, if you don't know who you are, the world is more than happy to provide you with a counterfeit identity. We are bombarded with false messages telling us that our identity can be found in material things like power, fame, sex, organizations, relationships, money, etc. Positions and titles may be roles we play; however, they are not the core of our identity. The problem with false identities is that when our identities are attached to our experiences, titles, achievements, or children, what happens if we lose a job, or the nest once filled with children empties? Who will you be then?

Our background, upbringing, and experiences may certainly influence and shape us, but our identities must be rooted in something more substantial. If not, life at best is frivolous. Jesus came so that we might experience life in its abundance. You don't have to settle for a cheap imitation of who and what God created you to be. You are designed by God with a unique blueprint. That blueprint contains everything that he has created you to be. The way to tap into that divine design is to find your true identity through Christ. As a believer you don't have to look further than the scriptures to find yourself.

Monarch Rule

Now it's your turn. Suppose you woke up tomorrow morning and discovered that you were not who you thought you were. Everything that you had known about your life, your status, and even your name and address, has changed. This new identity was that of a king. When you spoke, the universe hastened to your voice awaiting your command. Usually, kings were anointed with oil when rising to power. The anointing was a sacred act designed to empower the king to perform his duties by the power of the Holy Spirit. Bestowed upon him was a mantle and a staff which represented his authority. Sometimes a sword was placed in his hand. The sword would be used to defend, expand, and establish the king's territory.

As a child of God your true identity is as a king and priest on the earth. God has anointed and appointed you by the power of the Holy Spirit for your assignment. He has also given you the sword of the spirit which is the infallible word of God. The word is called a sword because it can be used offensively to thwart the attacks of the enemy. Additionally, it can be used defensively to counterattack your enemy. It is also by the word of God that your territory is established and defended.

Through Christ's finished work on the cross, an exchange was made in the restoration of sonship for those who choose to receive his sacrifice. While we are all created by God; however, we are not all God's children. The scriptures are clear that sonship is given to those who choose to accept the sacrifice that Jesus made for us on Calvary. Corinthians 5 lays the foundation for our identity in Christ. "Therefore if any man is in Christ he is a new creation. Old things pass away; behold, all things are become new." (2 Cor, 5:17 KJV) It also says that he gives those who receive him the right to become the sons of God. Therefore, our true identity is as the sons and daughters of God made in his image.

With that restoration we have been given all the covenant rights and benefits of sonship. "But ye are a chosen generation, a royal priesthood, an holy nation, a peculiar people; that ye should shew forth the praises of him who hath called you out of darkness into his marvellous light." (1 Pet. 2:9 KJV) Most kings rule by birthright. As born-again believers, we are the true royalty on the earth. But all too often we are not operating in our rightful seat of authority. This call to rule is a sovereign authority given to us by God. The time has come for the king's command and his decree to be executed. " For the earnest expectation of the creature waiteth for the manifestation of the sons of God." (Rom. 8:19 KJV)

At the point when you accept the sacrifice that Jesus made, repent of your sins, and verbally decree to ask him to become your Lord and saviour, a spiritual transaction takes place, and you are immediately translated from the kingdom of darkness into the kingdom of God. You are officially adopted into the family of God. However, breaking away from the residue of wrong mindsets and strongholds in your old life can be a process. Our minds are full of data from our experiences, the media, and all of the messages and voices that have influenced us. Sometimes the information on our hard drives doesn't align with the word of God.

Decrees can be an effective tool for reprogramming our mindsets. When used daily, decrees can train our minds and hearts to new truths. Changing a habit has to start with the revelation that there needs to be a change. Next, new thoughts must replace the old thought or habit. Meditating on the new thought helps to reinforce it until the old habit or mindset gives way to the new.

For years I struggled with my identity. On the outside I appeared confident and polished, but inwardly I was struggling with my identity. I read scriptures that said I was more than a conqueror and that I was seated in heavenly places with Jesus, but somehow those verses seemed so abstract. I read the bible and loved God, yet I struggled to believe all the things that God said that I was. I was the self-help guru reading every book I could find, and yet my life was a vicious cycle of successes followed by failure. One moment I was experiencing a mountain top victory only to find myself in the valley again.

Eventually, the Holy Spirit led me to a prayer book of affirmations. Every day I would confess the truth of who God said I was in his word. These simple affirmations revolutionized my life. Honestly, I was skeptical at first, and it appeared that nothing was happening. But after three days, the transformation had begun. I was actually beginning to believe what I was decreeing. I was also able to see myself as a child of God, special and beloved. The truth of how God saw me revolutionized my self-perception.

If you are going to step onto the landscape of the universe and make bold decrees, you must be certain of your identity. This level of kingly authority requires you to know who you are and understand your delegated authority. Most Christians are not walking in their authority and therefore are not ruling as God intended.

There are several critical reasons why identity is so important:

1. Identity Grants Access

Every morning, I waited in my car for a co-worker who had their badge to approach the door. Then I would run out of my car, hoping they would hold the door open for me. Even though I was a legitimate employee, without proper ID the door sensor would not recognize me or grant me access to the property. Just like having that ID badge, our identification with Christ grants us access to his blessings, benefits, power, and authority through our relationship with him. As a believer, your identification is found in Christ. There are certain rights and privileges that only come through union with Christ. Jesus said, "Behold I give you authority to tread on serpents and scorpions and over all the power of the enemy." (Luke 10:19 KJV)

2. Identity Determines Purpose

Floundering around to find your identity is a frustrating pursuit that can lead to unfulfillment. When you know who you are, it will determine the course of your destiny. Who I am governs the way that I approach life. Until you are certain of your identity, you won't be able to release your authentic voice. Identity is tied to purpose, authority, and voice. Once you know who and whose you are, it is then that you discover your purpose. Without being united to God you can't fulfill the destiny that he has for your life.

3. Identity Is Tied to Authority.

In Acts 19:15 "Some Jews who went around driving out evil spirits tried to invoke the name of the Lord Jesus over a man who was demon-possessed. They would say, 'In the name of the Jesus whom Paul preaches, I command you to come out.' One day the evil spirit answered them, 'Jesus I know, and Paul I know about, but who are you?' Then the man who had the evil spirit jumped on them and overpowered them all. He gave them such a beating that they ran out of the house naked and bleeding."(Acts 19:15 KJV).

This scripture demonstrates the reality that our identities have to be grounded in our union with Christ. That identity is the prerequisite for operating on earth and in the realm of the spirit. The question the demon asks is profound, because it is the question that we should be able to answer without any uncertainty. So, the question is, who are you? How do you define yourself? Those who belong to Christ are his true representatives. But if you don't know who you are, the devil will exploit you.

4. Identity Must Be Protected

Before he was conceived, Samson's parents were visited by an angel who revealed God's purpose for Samson. He was destined to become a judge over Israel and a Nazarite. No razor was to touch his hair, no strong drink was to be in his mouth, and he was forbidden to touch anything dead. But as Sampson grew, he began to relax the standards that God had established for his life. Additionally, his penchant for prostitutes eventually led to his demise. You can't study the life of Samson without asking how someone with such a miraculous birth could come to such a tragic end.

Nevertheless, there are two life lessons we can learn from Samson's epic failures:

1. *Holiness precedes power.*

Samuel plays with sexual immorality until it eventually costs him his position, his sight, and even his calling. Nobody likes to talk about sin anymore, but it is a reality. Playing with sin will short-circuit blessings and God's supernatural power in your life. You can't play with fire and expect not to get burned.

2. *Walk in absolute obedience.*

The blessings of God, although wonderful, require that we follow God's precepts and decrees. Each blessing is conditional. In Deuteronomy 28, God lays out the conditions for blessings. Those blessings are promised to those who obey God's decrees and precepts. Walking in authority requires that we are submitted to authority.

Our identification with Christ positions us to walk in authority. It is a privilege that requires us to remain vitally connected to God and in fellowship with him. Lamentations 3:37 says: "Who *is* he *that* saith, and it cometh to pass, *when* the Lord commandeth *it* not? It is God who grants us the authority and permission to speak to make decrees.

Jesus said in John 15:5: "I am the vine; ye are the branches. He that abideth in me, and I in him, the same bringeth forth much fruit; for without me you can do nothing. If a man remaineth not in me, he is cast forth as a branch, and withered; and men cast them into the fire, and they are burned. If you abide in me, and my words abide in you, ye shall ask what you will and it shall be done unto you."

Here Jesus makes a promise to his clinging branches. He says that if you remain in him and his words are a part of you, then you can ask, and it will be done. Identification requires that we first have a relationship with Christ and that we are abiding daily. Then the byproduct of that abiding relationship produces power to decree a thing and see it manifest.

PAUSE AND REFLECT

1. Who are you?

2. How would you describe yourself?

3. What messages have you received about your identity?

CHAPTER 4

The Power of Finding Your Voice

"Cry aloud! Don't spare! Lift up thy voice like a trumpet!..."

Isaiah 58:1 (KJV)

THE DOOR SLAMMED and from the glare in her eyes, I knew that I was looking into the face of evil. Yup, it was about to get ugly.

"I told you not to go back and tell your mother what goes on here," shouted Ms. Muse, with grey hairs peeking out from under her wig.

Just as her wig was used to cover her real locks, her plastic smile camouflaged her real motive—money. I was nothing more to her than a quick source of supplemental income. Once my mother left, I was locked away in solitary confinement in her private prison, a bedroom with a television. I was only released for bathroom breaks and lunch, and then I was quickly ushered back to "the cell." The slightest infraction received the maximum punishment of sentencing to "the chair." If sentenced to the chair, I would only be allowed to sit and look out the window.

My only defense was having a mother who had already begun empowering my voice. I knew to blow the whistle on any babysitter whose behavior was inappropriate. According to my records, Ms. Muse had committed several violations. When I reported to my mom how she was mistreating me, my mother confronted her. Unfortunately, I was the recipient of her vengeful backlash, which always resulted in Ms. Muse threatening me if I talked about what went on at her house. Despite her bullying I was determined she wasn't going to break me or shut me down. At the tender age of four, I had found my authentic voice and no cantankerous babysitter was going to steal it from me.

There are people like Ms. Muse who will use fear and intimidation to try to hijack your voice. There are even those who will offer a purchase price for your voice if you will just be silent. Your voice is a quintessential part of who you are; it is linked to your identity. Your voice can even reveal your personality by giving expression to your emotions and feelings. Each of us must find our own authentic voice. If you don't discover your true authentic voice, you won't be able to release your sound. Sound powers verbal decrees, declarations, and commands. Without discovering your voice, it is difficult to make a decree.

For years I knew there was an author lying dormant within me. As a child I was a library brat. My grandmother was a librarian, and it was on the floor of the children's department that God began to develop my love for books, words, reading, and writing. It was no surprise that in high school I gravitated towards English and excelled in writing. As an undergraduate, I majored in English and ended up teaching English. Even though I had been teaching people how to write for years, my own calling to write and my freedom to use my voice to express and decree through my writing had been stymied. I was undermined by people who scoffed at the idea of me writing, people who had no clue who I was or what I was called to. Attached to your gifting, there is a call. It took me years to realize that the enemy had used discouragement to silence my voice as a writer. It was as if a dark veil was cloaking that part of my voice that was to be released through writing.

My journey as an author began with releasing my voice and decreeing that I was who God created me to be—an author. I began to break the power of demonic decrees that had been spoken over me and my writing. I decreed best sellers, I decreed the pen of a ready writer, and the anointing to write. I decreed that my books would be published. What was I doing? I was overruling the schemes of the enemy to assassinate the writer that I was meant to be. I also stopped giving people backstage passes into my life who didn't genuinely have my best interests at heart. It has been absolutely liberating to finally walk in my destiny. You are reading this book today as a result of the campaign of decrees that I used to see this part of my ministry manifest.

Even as I write this, I am decreeing over you that you will find your unique voice and sound. I also decree that your sound which is critical to your unique destiny will be released. I decree that you will walk out your destiny. But it starts with finding and releasing your God-given inner voice. Please note that I said "God-given," because there are many voices, but we must discern those that are from God through the power of the Holy Spirit. There are voices coming from Satan and the world as well. In 1 Corinthians 14:10 it says, "There are, it may be, so many kinds of voices in the world, and none of them is without signification."

Every voice through its frequency has something it is transmitting.

We have to be very careful of the subtle ways that our voice can be silenced. Your voice can be threatened by:

The mountains of fear and intimidation.

The mountains of abuse, control, and toxic relationships and people.

The mountain of discouragement.

The mountain of compromise.

The mountain of sin.

The mountain of shame.

The mountain of poverty.

Voice is not just sound emitted from your voice box; it embodies the essence of the purpose behind the sound. Voice conveys the depth of your message, mission, suggestion, agenda, influence, vision, etc. Advertisers and the media understand the psychology of consumers and how the voice can be used as a powerful medium of influence. Products must have the ability to speak to the consumer. If a product doesn't speak to a customer, then no interest will be generated to drive sales.

Voice can also be conveyed through images and pictures that even without sound scream a distinctive message. Voice can be communicated very effectively through subliminal messages. Political groups also use the voice to echo their purpose. We can be programmed, conditioned, and indoctrinated through voice. Hitler used the power of his voice to hypnotize an entire nation, inciting them to acts of hatred and genocide.

Voice is further empowered when a voice is united with others, making the sound more powerful. God knew the power of voice when he decided that the people gathering to build the Tower of Babel had to be stopped. In Genesis 11:9: The Lord said, "If as one people speaking the same language, they have begun to do this, then nothing they plan to do will be impossible for them."

If one voice coupled with one vision and purpose was powerful enough to cause God to confuse the language of the builders, then think about how powerful your voice is.

Your voice is:

1. **Your unique sound. Don't be afraid of your own sound.**

2. **The power and permission from God to be you, not someone else's duplicate.**

3. **Intricately tied to your self-portrait. Our voices can often reveal our personalities.**

4. **Your God-ordained form of expression. Each of us is**

given individual talents and giftings.

Your gifting and your call are tied to your voice. So be yourself after you locate your true inner voice and decree out of that place. Your expression is tied to your sound. Some people are gifted with beautiful voices and the melodious sound that they release is part of their voice. If you are endowed with artistic abilities, that is part of your voice and expression. Others may be authors, dancers, mathematicians, doctors, or lawyers. Whatever God has called you to be, your voice is designed to be released into that sphere. Teachers are uniquely positioned to release their voice to decree over the students and the mountain of education. Nurses are able to decree over patients and the medical field in ways that others can't. God has us all stationed to release his voice through us in our own area of influence.

Your identity is everything that God created and intended you to be. This includes your background, upbringing, heritage. Don't ever let anyone steal your voice or shut you down. Your voice is the conduit for your sound. When you allow your voice to be silenced, you are essentially depriving the world of the gift that God has placed in you. Your story was meant to be told, someone is waiting for your invention, your song will be used by God to minister healing. Once you find your voice, God will help you to identify your tribe, people of like mind and thought. A tribe is a group of people whose voices are intrinsically distinctive, yet they share a common sound. That's why it is crucial for believers to stay connected to other believers who speak their language—"Jesus."

Before you can release your voice, you must first find it. Don't look for others to affirm your voice or what God has placed within you. Be vigilant when it comes to protecting this part of your identity.

One of the most freeing moments in my life was when I finally discovered my voice and began to sing my own song. I realized that the person God created me to be is more than enough. At this point in my life, I am unapologetically me. Also, whoever God creates us to be doesn't require someone else's consent or affirmation. Don't waste your time trying to fit into someone else's mold. If you are a child of God, that permission to be and decree comes from God alone. God has already given you permission to speak when he gave you the mandate to reign over the earth. Just be sure to align your voice with the frequency of heaven to ensure that the right sound is being released in the right season. You are already equipped with the acoustics, so use them.

PAUSE AND REFLECT

1. Have you found your authentic voice? If so, how are you releasing it?

   _____

   _____

   _____

   _____

2. Who or what has tried to silence your voice?

   _____

   _____

   _____

   _____

3. How are you sharing your unique God given gift with the world?

   _____

   _____

   _____

   _____

CHAPTER 5
Your Mountain Has Ears

"For most certainly I tell you, whoever may tell this mountain, 'Be taken up and cast into the sea,' and doesn't doubt in his heart, but believes that what he says is happening; he shall have whatever he says."

Mark 11:23 (Darby)

The Power of Sound

WE LIVE IN A WORLD that is activated by sound. The acoustics of the universe are wired to receive and transmit that sound through frequencies and vibrations. Nature is full of low and high frequency sounds. Birds all have distinct sounds and songs. Crackling fire makes its own distinct sound. The ocean roars as its waves crash. In outer space, radio waves pick up an orchestra of sounds in the galaxies. Scientists have also discovered that our DNA has a special code that produces a unique sound when put to music.

Everything around us communicates by its own special language. Language for humans translates into both sound and speech. However, not every sound that is released has the same meaning. For instance, when you hear the sound of an alarm clock it indicates that it's time to wake up. The sound of an ambulance siren signals an emergency that demands road clearance for medical responders. A mother learns to identify the various sounds of her baby's cry as a special language of expression.

God has wired mankind with the highest form of communication on earth. Only human intelligence is empowered with a voice to release complex language. God has assigned a specific sound to you through your unique voice that only you can release. The sounds of your voice are coded into your voice box to communicate a hierarchy of sound. We are all sound agents called by God to decree according to the dominion mandate. Everything in our universe is designed by God to respond to your voice. Whether we are aware of it or not, this dominion includes the spirit realm. God has created us to be over everything on earth, which means that disease, demons, principalities, situations, and circumstances are all waiting poised to hear what we will say, command, allow, or disallow.

Words on Assignment

For most of my childhood I suffered from allergies. I still have flashbacks of the eight shots every Friday at the allergy clinic. By my teens those allergies were all but gone. Then one day, while standing in my backyard talking to my neighbor about flowers, I blurted: "I love roses, but I am allergic to them." I couldn't believe the words coming out of my mouth. Why was I making that confession when I hadn't suffered with allergy symptoms for years? That night, after twelve years of being completely allergy-free, I woke up with itching hives all over my face. Instantly, I remembered the words I had spoken. The enemy had responded to my decree. Even though I had been healed, the spirit realm heard my new decree, and with my permission had responded by attacking me with allergy symptoms. This experience taught me the power of the spoken word. It also demonstrates how attentive the enemy is to our words. "Life and death truly are in the power of the tongue."(Prov. 18:24 KJV)

We must be very careful about the words we release into the material atmosphere. Because everything is voice-activated in our world.

There is creative power in our tongues. The tongue isn't just for tasting food and talking. It is a creative life force. God has given us dominion over the earth, but that dominion is released through the spoken word. Everything in earth's atmosphere is voice activated, created by the sound of words. This requires us to engage our territories and words with the spoken word of God. In other words, the tongue has the creative power to speak and create life. This should caution us to be very careful about what we say, because our words have infinite power. Many of the realities that we are experiencing today are the manifestation of words we have spoken in another season and that brought forth their life. Whether the words spoken are good or bad, they will always produce a harvest. Once words are released, they go to work in the atmosphere to create new realities.

Proverbs 18:21 confirms this truth by saying, "Death and life are in the power of the tongue, and those who love it will eat its fruits."

I had tapped into a principle that governs the universe. Whatever I said had the power to create a new reality. Once released, my words triggered a response and gave the enemy permission to activate sickness. We may be cavalier about what we say, but every word that comes out our mouth is released into the atmosphere on assignment. Think of words as arrows released and aimed at a particular target. Your words have purpose and are potent with power. Like God, we are made to engage this sound-activated world. Decrees are not just random; they are words on assignment. Word assignments are powered by sound. Spoken words release sound. Sound travels through the atmosphere. In fact, sound is such a powerful medium that it can unlock realms.

God didn't give any other species on earth the power of speech. Speech not only separates humans from other species by allowing us to function on a higher intellectual plane, it also empowers us to verbalize what is being processed in our minds. Remember you are empowered as the rightful ruler of the earth, and it's all in what you say. The reign of your territory includes everything that God has entrusted to you. As a representative of God's kingdom, I want to provoke you to open your mouth and legislate for the kingdom purposes of God. Each of us is called to action to effect change.

When to Use Decrees

So when should you use decrees? Use powerful decrees to establish justice in the land. Because we know that righteousness and justice are the foundation of God's throne, we don't have to have an epiphany to decree justice. Where you see poverty, decree provision. Where there is disease, decree health, healing and restoration. When men are dying in the street, we are charged to arise and issue prayer-filled decrees of life. I believe God wants us to use our decrees to restore his order on the earth. If our voices are silent, the rocks will cry out, but the rocks won't be accountable—we will.

The power to counteract the devices of the enemy lies within your mouth. With it we can bind the unrighteous acts of men. And with it, we can loose the heavens. God is calling us to decree not only for ourselves, but over generations and nations. Your decree can alter the landscape for the next generation. Even a song put to music can issue powerful declarations and decrees. Such sounds carry commands into the atmosphere. Many times, things remain stagnant because the sound is the same. A new sound can challenge and shift atmospheres to align with the purposes of God.

Your dominion authority was designed to be released through the power of what you say. Alter the course of your world with your voice and decree. Speak to the mountain that you are facing, because your mountain is not deaf it has ears, so speak to it.

PAUSE AND REFLECT

1. What sound have you been releasing?

_____

_____

_____

_____

2. What mountains do you need to speak to?

_____

_____

_____

_____

3. How are you using the powerful permission that God has given you to speak?

_____

_____

_____

_____

CHAPTER 6

Your Mountain is Calling

"Who are you, great mountain? Before Zerubbabel you are a plain;
and he will bring out the capstone with shouts of
'Grace, grace, to it!'"

Zechariah 4:7 (WEB)

Mountain Moments

WINDS WERE ROARING . . . coming at me and blowing from every direction. As I began speaking, the sound of my voice thundered with authority. To my aston-ishment, the winds were obeying and redirecting at my command. The landscape, atmospheric pressure, and elements began to change. Then I realized that I wasn't merely speaking to the wind, but to the hindering forces that were in operation behind them. I wasn't struggling to climb the mountain, I was on top of the mountain. The mountain top had become my command center.

My position in the dream symbolized my promotion to a new level of authority. It was now time for me to use the authority that God had given me.

God was using this dream to teach me that the power of my de-crees could truly subdue mountains. However, that power would have to be activated through my spoken words. A credit card gives us purchasing power, but an un-activated card can't be used to transact business. The power to transact and operate in the realm of the spirit must be activated by the voice of your authority as a believer. Nowhere in the bible does Jesus ever call us to climb mountains. He does, however, call us to speak to mountains, to conquer mountains, and to move mountains.

As you journey through life, you may encounter mountain experiences. I like to call them "mountain moments." These mountain moments are times when something that looks or feels like a giant mountain erects itself in your life. Mountains are the obstacles, failures, challenges, hindrances, disappointments, setbacks, demonic attacks, sicknesses, assaults, and crises that confront us. You step into a doctor's office only to come out with a life-threatening diagnosis. Your boss calls you into his office to inform you that you are being laid off. Some mountains harass and hinder us; other mountains threaten our families, security, peace, or finances.

Mountains can also form in our relationships, creating walls, barriers, and breaking down communication. While other mountains are man-made creations. Man-made mountains are created from choices we have made that have resulted in life challenges, such as debt we may have accumulated, or a mountain of addiction. Mountains can also be personal goals that you have set for yourself, like earning a degree, writing a book, purchasing a home, or starting a business. Oftentimes mountains are simply spiritual forces working to oppose you as a child of God. Whatever the situation, you have been challenged with a mountain moment.

When Mount St. Helens erupted in 1980, everyone was horrified. Although there had been minor tremors, no one expected the mountain volcano to erupt with a force that would leave debris miles away. Like Mount St. Helens, sometimes your mountain is more personal and internal. Internal emotional mountains can form within our hearts and minds. While on the surface everything may seem fine, taking a deeper look within would reveal a volcanic explosion just waiting to happen. Internal emotional tremors of depression, anger, rejection, bitterness, grief, pain, fear, and despair are internal volcanoes that threaten to erupt from within. The fallout from unresolved emotional mountains can leave a devastating trail of destruction in our own life and the lives of others.

For a season I was surrounded by an entire range of mountains threatening to engulf me. I was challenged by financial mountains, relationship mountains, and emotional mountains. I would issue a decree to one mountain and keep decreeing until it crumbled. But before I could rejoice for the victory, out of nowhere another mountain would form. That's when I learned that there is a decree for every mountain I will ever face. Simply find out what God has to say about your situation. Whatever scripture God leads you to becomes your decree. God's word will not return to him void.

When a mountain or obstacle forms in your life, don't waste time gossiping about the mountain or complaining about the problem. Jesus never told us to gossip or complain about the mountain. He told us to merely speak to the mountain. God requires us to release our faith and actively engage our enemy. When he said we could speak to a mountain and see it be removed, he didn't make any exceptions. So, it really doesn't matter what the mountain is for you to speak to it.

At some point in your life, you will have to face a mountain. Mountains are just part of the landscape of life. In fact, you may be facing a mountain this very moment as you read this book. Sometimes it's not just one mountain but a barrage of mountains that threaten to overtake you.

The question becomes what to do with the mountain you are facing. Every mountain demands a response. When your mountain calls, what will you do?

When a mountain presents itself in your life you have three options:

- Run from the mountain.

- Ignore the mountain.

- Stand and face your mountain.

No matter what mountain you are facing, there is a place of victory. How do I know? Because you are a mountain mover, and you are ensured victory. However, that victory starts in your mouth with what you decree to your mountain.

PAUSE AND REFLECT

1. What mountain are you facing right now?

   _____

   _____

   _____

   _____

2. Identify your mountain. Is your mountain financial? in your relationships?, health related?

   _____

   _____

   _____

   _____

3. How have you chosen to respond to the mountain?

   _____

   _____

   _____

   _____

CHAPTER 7

Mountain Movers Don't Fraternize with Fear

"For God has not given us the spirit of fear, but of power and love and a sound mind."

2 Timothy 1:17 (KJV)

The Snake Is Still Lying

MY HANDS CLUNG to the back of the truck's fender as it raced down the highway. It was the ride from hell. Waves of terror washed over me. How did I get here? Panic seized me and I knew that I couldn't hold on much longer. This scene was straight out of a horror movie and left me screaming to God for help.

Night after night I was plagued by this tormenting nightmare. The stress and challenges that I was facing during this season of my life left me feeling overwhelmed emotionally, financially, and physically. Although the challenges were real, the enemy was using those challenges to try to persuade me to agree with his fear tactics for my life. Whenever there is a challenging situation or circumstance, the spirit realm wastes no time moving in with doubt and fear in technicolor visuals.

It took some time, but eventually I realized that the dreams were just lies from the enemy. I also recognized that it was a lie that required my response and permission.

To launch my counterattack, I pulled Psalms 23 out of my arsenal and began to decree financial increase over my family. I started every morning decreeing that "The Lord is my shepherd" and that lack and want were not allowed in my life. Within one year of my Psalms 23 decree campaign, I watched God's provision manifest into a $15,000 raise, a new car, and money in my savings account. God also promises this:

"Verily I say unto you, Whatsoever ye shall bind on earth shall be bound in heaven: and whatsoever ye shall loose on earth shall be loosed in heaven."(Matt. 18:18 KJV). The word bind means to forbid with authority that is indisputable.

Once I decided that poverty was not allowed in my life, and began declaring increase and abundance, miracles happened. This was yet another turning point in my life, as I realized that the power of life and death were literally in my tongue. I began to decree not for the situation and what I was seeing but for what I wanted to see. As I began decreeing things began to happen. The results were absolutely shocking. Job 22 says: "You shall decree a thing and it shall be established for you."

Fear can be so debilitating that I decided to devote an entire chapter to overcoming it. Fear will keep you in a fetal position. It can shackle you so that you never step into the authority and destiny that God has granted you as his child.

It can also prevent you from walking through doors that God has opened for you. Additionally, it can make you mentally and physically sick and rob you of peace. Fear can also masquerade and present itself in many forms, including anxiety, panic, phobias, worry, dread, procrastination, insecurities, obsessions, and stress disorders.

The medical implications of fear can lead to accelerated aging, depression, premature death, gastrointestinal problems, infertility, a weakened immune system, and long-term memory impairment.

Here are some truths about fear:

1. **Fear-filled decrees are dangerous because if you decide to partner with fear it can alter your destiny.**

2. **Fear is the domain of Satan. Fear brings torment and Satan is the author of torment. Once we yield to fear it opens our minds to Satan's demonic projections.**

3. **Fear paralyzes, immobilizes, and arrests you.**

4. **Fear always demands to be center stage. Both faith and fear are leading actors, but fear will always try to upstage faith. Both of them can't share the limelight. Only one will dominate the stage of your life. Which leading actor has the center stage of your life right now—fear or faith?**

5. **Fear causes us to be irrational and it limits possibilities.**

6. **If you want to conquer fear you have to starve it to death and refuse to feed it. Whatever you feed will live; whatever you starve will die.**

7. **Decrees are found in the *no-fear zone*. Remember, when you step out to begin making bold decrees you are stepping into the no-fear zone.**

8. **Fear is usually laced with a lie. Look for the lie because a lie is a distortion of truth. I've learned that usually to find the truth all you need to do is reverse the lie.**

Satan's lies are nothing more than demonic decrees. When the enemy presents us with lies, we have to choose whether we will submit ourselves to those lies. You see, the minute the enemy comes knocking at the door of our lives, we can either empower his lies by agreement or simply shut those lies down with the truth found in God's word. You may be wondering, how can I do that? Most lies of the enemy are a perversion of God's truth. Find the scripture that speaks the truth about your situation and make war on the enemy by decreeing that scripture.

There really is tremendous power in agreement. The bible says that if two agree on anything they can have it. So many situations are created because we come into agreement with the devil. If we stand firm by resisting him with our authority and refuse to cooperate, he could not gain ground in our lives. When the devil attacks with his lies, it demands that you counterattack with the truth. The enemy may present you with false truth; however, you have the power to either reject or receive those lies. If the devil has cast a net of fear over your life, use your sword of the spirit—the word of God—to cut the net. Replace the lie of fear with the truth of the word. When you feel tempted to succumb to fear, never come into agreement with it. Refuse to give it permission to take hold in your mind. Scriptures admonish us to "be sober and vigilant because our enemy the devil is seeking whomever he can devour.

Walking by faith is a full-time occupation, and it demands that you cultivate a constant atmosphere of faith. Additionally, your faith-filled environment must be guarded and protected from those who would inject their doubts and fears. Even well-meaning people can be used by the enemy to send darts of fear to take the wind out of your sails and the air out of your balloon. Before you know it, people will have talked you out of your decree and replaced it with a decree of their own for your life.

Have none of it. Don't expect people to see what God has told or shown you. Moreover, you don't need the affirmation or permission of others if you are being empowered and led by the Holy Spirit. The bible says that two can't walk together unless they agree. Stop agreeing, entertaining, and fraternizing with fear. Instead, come into agreement with the seed that God has planted in your spirit. Mountain movers don't fraternize with fear. Surround yourself with those who are filled with faith. God has given to us all a measure of faith. Employ your faith and let it go to work arresting the fear in your life. Fear is nothing more than an outlaw and it's your job to arrest it and bring it into custody.

Faith-filled Decrees

In Matthew 14, the disciples are on a boat in the middle of the sea of Galilee:

After he had dismissed them, Jesus went up on a mountainside by himself to pray. Later that night, he was there alone, and the boat was already a considerable distance from land, buffeted by the waves because the wind was against it. At about three o'clock in the morning, the disciples are awakened by what they believed was an apparition of Jesus. When the disciples saw him walking on the lake, they were terrified. "It's a ghost," they said and cried out in fear. But Jesus immediately said to them: "Take courage! It is I. Don't be afraid." "Lord, if it's you," Peter replied, "tell me to come to you on the water." "Come," he said. Then Peter got down out of the boat, walked on the water and came toward Jesus. But when he saw the wind, he was afraid and, beginning to sink, cried out, "Lord, save me!" Immediately Jesus reached out his hand and caught him. "You of little faith," he said, "why did you doubt?" And when they climbed into the boat, the wind died down. Then those who were in the boat worshiped him, saying, "Truly you are the Son of God." (Matthew 14:22-35 KJV)

There are several principles that we can learn from this passage:

1. Fear thrives in a fear-filled atmosphere. You notice in the verse how they start out terrified, which sets the atmosphere for doubt and unbelief. Keep your environment charged with decrees of bold faith. Decreeing in the spirit requires an atmosphere charged with faith.

2. Faith is not stagnant, it moves; yet it's not fluid. When something is fluid it yields to external pressures. Faith is kinetic, but it doesn't yield itself to the circumstances. The boat was no longer near the shore, which meant the disciples had to launch out in deep waters. Only one disciple was bold enough to actually get out of the boat. If we want to operate in decrees, signs, wonders, and miracles, it will sometimes require us to step out and leave those who aren't willing to do it behind. Focus on the voice of the shepherd for guidance on how to align your words with his will. Deep Calls to Deep—so launch yourself out. Faith always requires that we take action. Fear will keep you from launching out. Faith moves forward.

3. Our faith has been designed to be tested and promoted. Romans 1:17 says, "We go from faith to faith." This means that the possibilities of increasing in faith are limitless. Peter's sinking reveals his level of faith. Although he had enough faith to step out, he didn't have the level of faith required to walk on the water. We see Jesus operating in the full measure of faith in contrast to Peter, who was fearful. Each believer is given a measure of faith, but faith must continue to grow, develop, and advance.

4. Faith must remain anchored to God. When God ceases

to be the source of our faith, we enter the danger zone.

5.   **Most of the things that are causing us fear, stress, and anxiety God has already taken care of. When I look back on all the frightening mountains that I've had to face, it's so easy to see that while I was stressing out, God had already solved the problem. All of that sense-less fretting, when all you have to do is trust a loving father who has every nuance of your life preplanned.**

Twelve spies were commissioned by Moses to spy out the land of Canaan. Of the twelve, only two mountain movers (Caleb and Joshua) came back and decreed: "Let us go up at once and take possession, for we are well able to overcome it."

But the men who had gone up with him said, "We are not able to go up against the people, for they *are* stronger than we." And they gave the children of Israel a bad report of the land which they had spied out, saying, "The land through which we have gone as spies *is* a land that devours its inhabitants, and all the people whom we saw in it *are* men of *great* stature. There we saw the giants (the descendants of Anak came from the giants); and we were like[b] grasshoppers in our own sight, and so we were in their sight." (Num. 13:30-33 KJV)

What happens next is one of the most tragic scenes in the bible. Outraged at their lack of faith and bad report, God decreed that the Israelites would wander in the wilderness for forty years because they weren't willing to take the land. Moreover, the entire generation of men who left Egypt during the Exodus would die in the desert, except for Joshua and Caleb who did not slander the promises of God.

Fear is simply not an option, because God has commanded us not to be afraid. There are good reasons why we can't afford to entertain fear. To move in bold decrees, you can't listen to the fearful. Silence the voices of naysayers. Use your energy to fuel your faith. When you boldly step out to take a step of faith God will meet you.

God has called us to operate in several realms. One of those realms is the realm of faith; however, we can't walk in the realm of faith-filled decrees if we are bound by fear. In earlier chapters I talked about some of the prerequisites for operating in the realm of decrees. Fear is the exact opposite of faith. It will limit your ability to govern and rule in the spirit realm and operate in legislative authority. Legislative authority requires us to use our decrees.

Fear factors God right out of the equation. In Mark 11:23, when talking to his disciples Jesus said:

"For verily I say unto you, That whosoever shall say unto this mountain, Be thou removed, and be thou cast into the sea; and shall not doubt in his heart, but shall believe that those things which he saith shall come to pass; he shall have whatsoever he saith."(Mark 11:23 KJV)

Our worlds are framed by the words we speak. Whenever things in your life are not in alignment with the word of God, *use the power of decrees crafted from the word of God to reframe your world.*

When we see situations that don't align with God's perspective, God has given us the power to speak. When we release words, the unseen realm is waiting to respond to the command. We must see words not just as mere syllables, but as having the power to legislate in the realm of the spirit. Legislate is a legal term that means to make rules or laws concerning certain activities.

Just as the spoken word is used in a court of law by judges to render verdicts, the spoken word of a Christian in right relationship with God carries the weight to render verdicts on earth and in the spirit realm. The bible calls us kings and priests and tells us that we are more than conquerors. You are not a mere victim of circumstance. It doesn't matter if you've been in a cycle of failure and disappointment. God has empowered you to effect change in your territory and realm of influence. Open your mouth and begin speaking. Mountains may form in front of you, but you have authority over mountains and obstacles. There is deliverance in the word of God. It is sharper and more powerful than any sword, trumping all other swords in the universe. Nothing that Satan has in his arsenal can stand against it. That means that your mountain is not impregnable.

Once the mountain of fear is removed in your mind, everything becomes possible. In case you didn't know, you are a mountain mover. Get ready to move those mountains out of your way.

PAUSE AND REFLECT

Ask God to expose any lies that have been operating in your life. Also, be intentional about feeding your faith.

1. Which mountains are causing you the most fear and anxiety right now?

_____

_____

_____

_____

2. How have you been fraternizing with fear?

_____

_____

_____

_____

3. What have you been doing to feed your faith?

_____

_____

_____

_____

CHAPTER 8

Mountain Moving Strategies

"Who are you, great mountain? Before Zerubbabel thou shalt become
a plain: and he shall bring forth the headstone thereof with shoutings,
crying, Grace, grace unto it.you are a plain; and he will bring out the
capstone with shouts of 'Grace, grace, to it!'

Zechariah 4:7 (KJV)

David's Decree

ONE OF THE FIRST BIBLE stories I learned in Sunday school as a
little girl was the story of David and Goliath. The story of a young boy
flinging his slingshot who, by some twist of fate, hits his enemy straight
between the eyes. Everyone loves the story of an underdog emerging victorious when the odds are ridiculously stacked against him. It may appear that David's victory was won when he hit Goliath with the smooth
stone. However, upon closer examination, it's evident that David's victory began long before his showdown with Goliath. In fact, David had
already been anointed king when the enemy began trying to silence his
voice.

The first scene of this historic battle in I Samuel 17:10 opens with
the champion Goliath charging out of the Philistine camp looking for
a man to fight. Goliath the Philistine says, "I defy the armies of Israel

this day: give me a man that we may fight together." He is calling for a man to come to fight. Of all the men in Israel, only the inexperienced David steps forward. The question you have to ask is, why didn't King Saul defend his territory? Why was a teenager standing to defend Israel?

The opposition begins when David steps out to decree the word of the Lord over a national crisis: " Eliab his oldest brother heard when he spoke to the men; and Eliab's anger was kindled against David, and he said, "Why camest thou down hither? and with whom hast thou left those few sheep in the wilderness? I know thy pride, and the naughtiness of thine heart; for thou art come down that thou mightest see the battle? "David said, "What have I now done? Is there not a cause?" He turned away from him toward another, and spoke like that again; and the people answered him again the same way."

(1 Sam.17:28-30 KJV)

When God has given you permission to speak, no one can silence you. While everyone else was just watching the confrontation with Goliath, David arises empowered with a bold decree in his mouth that shifts the battle. David's persistent inquiry leads to the first bold decree that he makes to King Saul: "David said to Saul, "Let no man's heart fail because of him. Your servant will go and fight with this Philistine." (Samuel 17:32 KJV)

What David said was overheard and reported to King Saul, who sent for him. "David said moreover, The Lord that delivered me out of the paw of the lion, and out of the paw of the bear, he will deliver me out of the hand of this Philistine." And Saul said unto David, "Go, and the Lord be with thee."(1 Sam.17:37 KJV)

David stood facing Goliath with one smooth stone that he used to combat the champion. Nobody even knew who David was, and yet he was boldly making his decree of faith. I have read this verse a thousand times, but I had overlooked the powerful decree that David makes. David's victory started not when he gathered the five smooth stones, but when he began issuing powerful decrees. If you really want to see a shift in your circumstances, you have to realize that the victory is in your mouth. It all starts with what you are decreeing. David's final decree is:

"Thou comest to me with a sword, and with a spear, and with a shield: but I come to thee in the name of the Lord of hosts, the God of the armies of Israel, whom thou hast defied.

This day will the Lord deliver thee into mine hand; and I will smite thee, and take thine head from thee; and I will give the carcases of the host of the Philistines this day unto the fowls of the air, and to the wild beasts of the earth; that all the earth may know that there is a God in Israel.

And all this assembly shall know that the Lord saveth not with sword and spear: for the battle is the Lord's, and he will give you into our hands."(1 Sam.17:45-47 KJV)

David boils with holy indignation and rises to the challenge. Not once does he cower as he takes on the seasoned champion warrior. As we examine this verse, we typically view David from the perspective of an impulsive boy who gets lucky fighting a giant. However, there are several key factors that sealed Goliath's fate and David's success:

1. **David had already been chosen and anointed by God.**

In 1 Samuel 16:1," God says to Samuel: "..I will send thee to Jesse the Bethlehemite: for I have provided me a king among his sons."

Without a doubt, David had been chosen by God and God was with him. The battlefield is no place for children. David didn't step onto the battlefield as a boy but as a king. He was operating in that kingly anointing. He was fully empowered by the Holy Spirit for his challenge. From the moment he was anointed the Spirit of the Lord came powerfully upon David. In verse 13 we see the power, the presence, and the Holy Spirit of God descending on David but departing from Saul.

2. God was with David.

What did David have that Goliath didn't? The God factor. Romans 8:31: "If God is for us, who can be against us?"

David wasn't just victorious because of his slingshot or any chosen stones. David's secret to success was the fact that God was with him. David's intimate relationship with God is evidenced by his pure worship of God. This principle can be applied to any giant that you may be facing. John 15:7 states: "If ye abide in me, and my words abide in you, ye shall ask what ye will, and it shall be done unto you."

God is the source of all power. Therefore, staying vitally connected to him in an abiding relationship ensures his power, victory, and presence in your life. Any giant that comes against you will also be opposing God if you are his child. I have watched enemies rise up against me, and each time, I have witnessed the power of God. It used to upset me when enemies would launch attacks against me. Now I just pop the popcorn, pull up a good seat, and watch my dad finish the fight. He has never lost a battle. Of course, that doesn't mean that I don't have to pick up my weapons and do my part to fight. It does mean that I never have to fight alone, and my victory is always guaranteed. "Now thanks be unto God, which always causeth us to triumph in Christ, and maketh manifest the savour of his knowledge by us in every place." (2 Cor. 2:14 KJV)

If you face an enemy, the hosts of heaven are mobilized to fight on your behalf. Rest in the victory that Jesus has secured in his finished work on the cross.

3. David issued a decree.

These weren't just haphazard words, but words from the one who was anointed as king with the authority to speak victory and deliverance over his territory. David's decrees were released boldly from the position of his kingly anointing and authority. More importantly, it was also the by-product of the confident security of David's abiding relationship with God.

4. David's decrees are strategic.

In order for decrees to be effective they must be strategic. Along with stating his decrees, David strategically releases a smooth stone that hits the intended target. David could have chosen any stones. However, he chose five smooth stones. David's smooth stone increases the odds of accuracy. Stones with rough edges would've been more resistant to sailing smoothly through the air. Every circumstance in life requires strategic maneuvering. However, dismantling a mountain requires strategy and proper tools.

Strategies for Taking Down a Mountain

When you are faced with a mountain. You will either rise to the challenge to defeat your mountain or cower in fear and succumb to the mountain. If you decide to advance, you will need a strategy and the right tools in order to prevail.

When conquering mountains, the following strategies need to be considered:

Strategy #1: Develop a Mountain Mover's Perspective.

Mountain movers aren't born, they are made. That means that you can become a mountain mover. Mountain movers have a different perspective. Mountain movers see themselves as conquerors. Remember, Caleb and Joshua, out of all the spies, believed that they were more than able to overcome. A mountain is a mountain; it really doesn't matter the size or kind. Don't look at the size of the giant you're facing; instead, focus on the giant living on the inside of you. That Giant is Jesus Christ.

Strategy #2: Develop a Vision of Victory.

What would victory look like with the mountain that you are facing? Maybe it's living in complete financial freedom liberated from the tyranny of consumer debt. Or it could be a new you, thirty pounds lighter. Whatever the challenge, write down your vision of victory on the other side of that challenge and picture it in your mind. Keep that vision before you and let it spur you on to your victory.

Strategy #3: Identify Your Mountain.

Identifying your mountain demystifies the abstract challenge you may be facing. An opponent that you can't see or can't recognize ensures defeat. Sometimes it may require asking help from people with a professionally trained eye to assist you in identifying a problem. Such as a licensed therapist or a pastor. When my daughter was having challenges in school, I knew there was a problem; I just wasn't sure what it was. I hired an educational consultant and with her expertise we were able to address several problems. Other times there are underlying root issues that have to be addressed. Identifying the problem is half the battle.

MOUNTAINS HAVE EARS: "SPEAK TO THEM"

Strategy #4: Devise Your Strategy.

Strategize, strategize, strategize. Partner with the Holy Spirit and ask him to guide you. God knows which strategy to employ in every situation. Sometimes the strategy is obvious. At other times it may require action to be taken, like making a phone call, waiting patiently, carefully planning, gathering information, or just listening to the voice of God.

Strategy#5: Launch the Right Weapon.

Find the scripture solution to your problem. God has already addressed any issue we could ever face in life. Once you know what the bible has to say about your situation, you can begin to think about the decree that speaks to your circumstances. Sometimes you may receive a word of knowledge or a prophetic word that can be used to decree. Other times, the logos word (scripture) may be used. However, all decrees must align with the principles found in the word of God. Jesus gives us the perfect model in John 12:49 where he said: " For I have not spoken of myself; but the Father which sent me, he gave me a commandment, what I should say, and what I should speak." Likewise, we aren't speaking on our own with decrees. We are saying expressly what aligns with what God has said.

Strategy #6: Cast down imaginations that oppose the word of God.

You must wage war against thoughts that would sabotage your decrees. That also includes emotions. You can't move in the realm of bold decrees if you live in your feelings. Honestly, there will be some days when you won't feel like mountain moving. But when something is decomposed, its elements are separated into smaller parts. If you reduce your mountain to its lowest common denominator, that means that you are only speaking to rocks and dust. Something changes in your psyche when you have a paradigm shift in your perceptions. Sometimes the real dismantling that needs to occur is in the dismantling of our own of strongholds, systemic ideologies, and mindsets. Once the mountain loses its size and grandeur, fears subside, and reality tames distortions. Now with the power of God and his word, you can begin to see yourself as a victor. You are equipped to conquer the mountain rather than being victimized by the mountain.

Strategy #7: Use Your Sword and Your Scepter.

David's mountain moment took place in the form of a giant by the name of Goliath. His mountain was nine feet tall and tormented the Israelites day and night. Goliath was a skilled warrior who had been in fighting from his youth. David is a shepherd boy who has never seen a single military battle, yet he defeats Goliath. He uses his stones and his kingly authority. Remember David has already been anointed as king over Israel. To defeat a mountain you need to use the sword of the spirit and the scepter of your kingly authority.

Strategy #8: Forge Your Decrees in Prayer.

Goliath came against David with weapons of the flesh, but David was wielding weapons that had been forged in the spirit. Forge your decrees in prayer, allowing the Holy Spirit to fill your mouth with the Rhema word. Decrees birthed in prayer become a weapon of destruction against the enemy and his forces. Spend time praying so that the Holy Spirit can show you the strategy. If necessary, set aside a time of fasting and prayer to seek God for your unique battle plan.

Strategy #9: Conquer Your Personal Goliaths.

Goliath is the obstacle that stands between you and your destiny. Before David could step across the threshold of destiny, he had to slay his Goliath. Little did he know that his bold decrees and faith would serve as the catalyst to usher him into his destiny. Sometimes right before the breakthrough, the promotion, the healing, the battle intensifies. The bible warns us not to be ignorant concerning Satan and his devices. The strategy of the enemy is to try to abort the dream God has given you before it can take flight. However, if the enemy can't stop you, he will try to harass, distract, and derail you. Dare to step out in your kingly anointing and speak to the Goliaths in your life. Don't be shaken by any enemy that is challenging you. Why? Because the power of the king's decree can alter situations and nullify satanic schemes.

It doesn't matter what mountain has formed against you, there is a faith-filled decree that can bring it down. I am a firm believer that God allows certain mountains to touch our lives not only to draw us closer to him, but to teach us to conquer and prevail. We aren't called to be mere mountain climbers, but mountain movers.

PAUSE AND REFLECT

1. What strategies has the enemy been using to try to defeat you?

_____

_____

_____

_____

2. Prayerfully ask the Holy Spirit to reveal the strategy for victory. What strategy do you need to employ to align with your decree?

_____

_____

_____

_____

3. Do you have a mountain mover's perspective? If not, what needs to change?

_____

_____

_____

_____

4. Develop a vision for victory. What would victory look like for you?

_____

_____

_____

_____

CHAPTER 9
Enforcing Your Decree

"All the presidents of the kingdom, the governors, and the princes,
the counsellors, and the captains, have consulted together to establish
a royal statute, and to make a firm decree, that whosoever shall ask a
petition of any God or man for thirty days, save of thee,
O king, he shall be cast into the den of lions."

Daniel 6:7 (KJV)

MY GOLIATH wasn't a nine-foot giant. It was a champion university threatening that I would not graduate on time. Every night, I would wake up to stand on the floor of the universe to issue my decree that I would graduate that year. Like the persistent widow, I continued meeting with the counselor at the school to try to find a solution. After the third meeting, the counselor told me there was no hope of me graduating. I left the school and as I walked out to my car I remember feeling so discouraged. I heard the voice of God say to me, "It's not faith until it's tested. If you've issued your decree, why are you shaken because the school is saying no? Are you going to stand or allow the enemy to silence your decree?"

That night I rose again, and again, and again to issue the same decree—that I would graduate and that no weapon formed against me would prevail. Finally, one day after work while on the way to my car, my phone rang. It was my counselor, who had found a way for me to graduate on time. My persistence in decreeing had changed the landscape. I am convinced that there are some breakthroughs that without decreeing we simply are not going to see. It doesn't matter how impossible the circumstances may appear. "For we walk by faith and not by sight."

Sometimes we must enforce our decrees and keep enforcing them until they come to pass. Enforcing this particular decree required persistence and bulldog tenacity. Luke 18:1-8 tells the story of a widow's persistence that yielded results:

"And there was a widow in that city; and she came unto him, saying, 'Avenge me of mine adversary.' And he would not for a while; but afterward he said within himself, 'Though I fear not God, nor regard man; Yet because this widow troubleth me, I will avenge her, lest by her continual coming she weary me.' And the Lord said, 'Hear what the unjust judge saith. And shall not God avenge his own elect, which cry day and night unto him, though he bears long with them? I tell you that he will avenge them speedily. Nevertheless, when the Son of man cometh, shall he find faith on the earth?'" (Luke 18:8 KJV)

From the time you issue your Holy Spirit empowered decree, it is already a done deal in the realm of the spirit. However, that doesn't mean your authority may not be challenged by the enemy and life circumstances. Sometimes when you step out to make a decree it manifests quickly. But there are times when you step out to issue your decree and the battle intensifies. It's tempting during such times to doubt the validity of the word of God and the power of the decree. But take heart, this is not the time to withdraw your decree. Hebrews 10:35 warns us not to "So do not throw away your confidence; it will be richly rewarded." We can't afford to relent in our decree, because our families, communities, churches, businesses, ministries, and nations are hinged upon the way in which we legislate on the earth.

The caller recounted the scene to the 911 dispatcher. The suspect had just violently attacked her son. There was no doubt in the mind of the police that this was their guy. The officer had spotted him wandering around a child daycare center. He was still wearing the blood-stained shirt from the crime scene. The officer approached the suspect and told him to get down on the ground. When the suspect refused, the officer issued the command again, and when the suspect refused, he tased him. The suspect fell to the ground but sprang back up on his feet, pulled his knife, pointed it at the officer and threatened to use it. The officer tased him again and finally after some resistance, he was able to take the man into custody.

Although the officer had authority and had issued a series of commands, he was met with resistance. Everybody knows that the police are **empowered** with authority. So, the question becomes, why would an officer of the law with legitimate authority have to enforce a command? The answer is simple: some criminals are compliant, while others won't be taken down without a fight. The word "enforce" is defined as the process of ensuring compliance with laws, regulations, rules, standards, and social norms. The root word of enforce is "force." Which means strength or power exerted upon an object. Just like the police officer, the authority of the believer is never in question because it is authentic. Therefore, the resistance of the enemy in no way diminishes our authority or the power of our decrees. Think of it this way, when a law is enacted it comes with the full weight of the governing authorities in the land. The minute the law is signed it becomes an official edict and is enacted. However, there may be citizens in the land who refuse to adhere to the law that has been decreed. When citizens don't comply, another sector of the judicial system must be utilized—law enforcement. The police officer may be armed with tasers, guns, batons, etc. However, the bible tells us that the weapons of our warfare are not physical or carnal, but spiritual through

God to pull down strongholds. Don't hesitate to use the spiritual weapons God has provided to enforce your decree.

How to Enforce Your Decree

Enforce your decree by doing the following:

1. Pray and decree with persistence.

The most powerful weapon in the believer's arsenal is still prayer. When you pray you are tuning into the frequency of heaven. Just as you have to tune in to a specific station on the radio in order to listen. Tuning into God in prayer requires us to connect with him to communicate. Noise and static in your prayer life will make it difficult to commune with God. Bold decrees must be coupled with persistent prayer.

As you stand in prayer the Holy Spirit will guide you with promptings, scripture, words of knowledge, an impression, prophecy, or maybe just a still quiet voice. Thank God in advance for all that he is doing in your situation.

2. Wage war with your decree.

At times you may have to use your decree as a weapon of war to enforce the release of demonic interference. But don't give up or lose heart. Keep decreeing. You may wonder why there would be any opposition if you're operating in your kingly anointing as a child of God. The answer is found in Ephesians 6:12:

"For we wrestle not against flesh and blood, but against principalities, against powers, against the rulers of the darkness of this world, against spiritual wickedness in high places."(KJV)

Your authority may be challenged by rebellious despots in the universe. But don't give up or lose heart. Keep decreeing. Take authority over situations and speak directly to them as if they were mountains.

3. Don't allow the enemy to silence your decree.

Recall that in chapter four we talked about the voice snatchers who will try to silence your voice or declaration. Don't relinquish your authority to the enemy by allowing him to silence your decree. Open your mouth and decree. The universe awaits your command.

4. Release your faith.

Expect that your decree will manifest. Remember, it isn't a matter of "if" but "when" it will happen. Settle in your heart and mind that your decree has been established and that it will come to pass. Again, keep in mind that we are talking about decrees aligning with the will of God. So it's important to be sensitive to God's timing. Sometimes God is working on our behalf according to a big plan that we just can't see. Be patient with the process.

5. Prepare and position yourself.

So many times, I have decreed something and when it came to pass, I wasn't prepared for it. Carefully consider what you are really asking God for. If you are decreeing you will have a new job, get your resume ready, buy a suit, etc. If your decree is for a house, you need to take the steps of saving money, monitoring your credit, and looking at homes. Or for instance, if you are decreeing to pass an exam, you will have to study. Don't neglect the practical application.

6. Decree it until you see it.

Keep decreeing. God has given us the keys to the kingdom and one of those keys is to use decrees. Remember to decree it until you see it manifest. Persistence like the widow's pays off. Continue decreeing despite opposition or **n**ot seeing results. The bible says that we walk by faith, not by sight. (2 Corin. 5:7) As you decree, your words are creating things in the unseen realm. Stand firm until the desired decree transitions from the unseen realm and enters this realm to become your reality.

7. When necessary, use spiritual and natural resources.

Some verbal decrees will need to be coupled with natural reinforcements. In certain situations, enforcing your decree may require you to take action. Don't be afraid to use the court system, make phone calls, etc. Do the practical things that may be necessary.

Enforcing decrees is one facet of exercising our authority as believers. If you are met with resistance or have grown weary in the waiting, don't relent. Enforce your decrees through prayer, faith, and persistence and watch God manifest your miracle.

PAUSE AND REFLECT

1. Who or what has tried to silence your decree?

_____

_____

_____

_____

2. What do you need to do to enforce your decree?

_____

_____

_____

_____

CHAPTER 10
Issue Your Decree

"I will declare the decree: the Lord hath said to me...."

(Psalm 2:7 KJV)

OUR WORLDS ARE FRAMED by the words we speak. Whenever you reach a place where things in your life are not in alignment with the word of God, use the power of your words to reframe your world. We must regard words not as casual syllables but as active forces with the power to legislate in the realm of the spirit. Words hold the power to legislate in the spiritual realm, just as the spoken word is used in a court of law by judges to render verdicts.

Wherever you find yourself, whatever the reality of your present world, it can be changed by the power of your decree. If you really want to move your mountain, it starts with what you say. We have reached the point in our journey where it is now time for you to issue your decree. It's time for you to take the authority Christ has given to you and use it. Arise now and release the voice that God has given you to rule and reign. Don't wait another day to activate your decrees.

The decrees that I have included in this part of the book are meant to be like training wheel prayers to give you a start. Once you get going, allow the Holy Spirit to guide your decrees in the name of Jesus. At the end of the chapter, I have left blank pages for you to draft your own Holy Spirit inspired decrees. Employ these decrees and let them go to work for you in your life. Remember, your new life is like a blank canvas, but your vision can't be painted without a brush. Get ready to activate the spoken word of God. Decree like an artist with a paintbrush to co-create a new scene for your life. Your life will never be the same.

MOUNTAIN DECREES

Prosperity and Provision

Mastering Your Mind

Divine Health

Your Identity in Christ

Decreeing Your Authority

The Mountain of Fear

Declaring Victory

Salvation

Prosperity and Provision

"The Lord is my shepherd; I shall not want."

Psalms 23:1 (KJV)

THE PSALMS 23 DECREE

This decree requires that we catch the revelation of the God who is the source of everything. Everyone on earth is striving for the resources that originate not on Wall Street, but from the throne room of heaven. Once we have the right mindset, we understand that the root of "resource" (which basically means provision) is the word "source." Remember that a partner, a job, a degree, a bank account, investments, or businesses are not your source. God is the source of every resource. If the source of blessing dries up, God is more than able to provide. Elijah had become dependent on a brook of provision that suddenly dried up. Like Elijah, we can also become too reliant on a particular stream of blessing. Just when we become overly dependent on one source, God will sometimes change the geographical location of that provision. This is to ensure that we realize that he alone is the provider.

Lay hold of the Psalms 23 decree: "The Provision of the Shepherd."

The Lord is my Shepherd, and I shall not want . . . Don't just contemplate and recite the words of Psalms 23. Make it your own.

Issue Your Decree of Prosperity & Provision

In Jesus's name:

I decree that the Lord is my shepherd, and I will not experience any poverty or lack.

I decree that I excel in all that I put my hand to. No weapon of poverty that has been formed against me shall prosper.

I decree that I shall not want for peace, joy, prosperity, healing, promotion, favor, or blessing.

I decree that I am a faithful steward and that the devourer is rebuked from my finances.

I decree that the windows of heaven are opened over me and I don't have room for all the blessings.

I am prospering in every area of my life even as my soul prospers.

Every one of my needs are met according to your riches in glory.

I am the head and not the tail. I am above only and not beneath. I am the landlord not the renter, the lender not the borrower.

I decree the wisdom to steward finances.

I decree that not only do I work for my money, but my money works for me.

I decree increase, abundance, and wealth. I decree wealth transfers and releases. I decree abundance, multiplication, and addition of benefits in my life.

I excel in all that put my hand to. I am loaded daily with God's benefits.

I decree that my businesses and ventures are prosperous.

The blessing of the Lord makes me rich and he will add no sorrow to it.

MASTERING YOUR MIND

"Finally, brethren, whatsoever things are true, whatsoever things are
honest, whatsoever things are just, whatsoever
things are pure, whatsoever things are lovely, whatsoever things are of
good report; if there be any virtue, and if there be any praise, think on
these things."

Philippians 4.8 (KJV)

The mind is the command center of the body. This is the area of intellect in the brain where reasoning goes on and judgments and decisions are made. The mind has been charged with the task of leading the rest of the body. The mind is also the central warehouse for our thoughts and imagination.

Place a sentinel around your thoughts and guard them well, because everything is first conceived as a thought. That's why it is critical to discern thoughts that are not aligned with the word of God. When such thoughts arise, the time to master a thought is when it first presents itself.

"**Casting** down imaginations and every high thing that exalts itself above the knowledge of God."(2 Cor. 10:5 KJV). Use these decrees daily to help you master your thoughts and mind.

Issue Your Decree for Your Mind

In Jesus's name:

I take authority over my mind, thoughts, and emotions.

I decree that I have the mind of Christ. I meditate on things that are true, noble, just, pure, lovely.

I set watch over my mind and reject all lies presenting as truth.

I renew my mind so that I am not conformed to this world but transformed by the daily renewal of my mind through the word of God.

My mind is set and fixed on things in heaven above, not on the things of this earth.

I cast down every thought that doesn't conform to the word of God.

I apply the blood of Jesus to cleanse my mind of every negative thought.

I decree that every generational pattern of negative thinking, curses, mental illness, confusion, pride, rebellion, error, depression, anxiety, and fear are broken.

I decree that I don't lean to my own understanding, but that I am led by the Holy Spirit.

My mind and memory are sharp. I have the skill, wisdom, and understanding of Daniel.

I break agreement with every mindset and stronghold, and decree a complete renovation of my thoughts.

DIVINE HEALTH

"But he was wounded for our transgressions, he was bruised for our iniq-
uities: the chastisement of our peace was upon him; and with his stripes
we are healed."

Isaiah 53:5 (KJV)

Walking in divine health is God's health care plan for us. Yet there are
several facets to health. In 3 John 2, the apostle John says: "" Beloved
above all things I wish that you will prosper and be in good health even
as your soul prospers." From the verse it's apparent that prospering
means not only good physical health but also the soul's health. Divine
health is a combination of a healthy spirit, mind, body, and emotions.
Negative emotions like anger, depression, anxiety, bitterness, and stress
can cause health challenges. Unforgiveness and bitterness can alter our
bodies at the cellular level, weaken our immune systems, and make it
difficult to ward off diseases.

Oncologists are now making the connection between the inabil-
ity to forgive and cancer. In fact, some doctors are asking their cancer
patients if there is anyone they need to forgive. The sin of unforgiveness gives Satan the legal right to attack our bodies with sickness.

If you are challenged with the mountain of sickness or disease,
refuse to come into agreement with the diagnosis. Don't own it, don't

agree with it, and don't tolerate it. Know that you wrestle from a position of authority. Issuing a decree for divine health requires us to use our authority. You aren't asking or begging for healing, you are enforcing the healing that is already yours. The purchase price for that healing was paid in full by Jesus on the cross. Healing is your covenant right as a child of God.

Issue Your Decree for Divine Health

Before making this decree pray and ask the Holy Spirit if there is anyone you need to forgive.

In Jesus's name:

I decree that according to Isaiah 53:5 that by Jesus's stripes I am healed.

I decree that my body functions according to God's divine blueprint.

I apply the blood of Jesus to my mind and body. I declare healing from all trauma, drama, and rejection. My emotions are whole and I am healed in the spirit of my mind.

I walk in forgiveness and choose to release those who have wronged me so that I give no place to the devil.

I bind all sickness and disease and forbid it to operate in my body.

I command every organ, cell, limb, and system to function in divine order.

I cancel the assignment of the enemy and the power of every demonic diagnosis.

I decree that no weapon of sickness or disease that has been formed against me shall prosper.

I release resurrection power over my body, and I decree signs, wonders, and manifestations of healing in Jesus's name.

YOUR FAMILY

"And if it seem evil unto you to serve the Lord, choose you this day
whom ye will serve; whether the gods which your fathers served that
were on the other side of the flood, or the gods of the Amorites, in whose
land ye dwell: but as for me and my house, we will serve the Lord."

Joshua 24:15 (KJV)

When it comes to praying for your family the best strategy is to be led by
the Holy Spirit and to lay up prayer. Prayer is just simply talking to God.
Don't wait for something to happen, stay on the offensive. The bible says
that a good man leaves an inheritance for his children's children. We
should leave natural assets to our children; but be careful not to neglect
your spiritual heritage and legacy. A hedge of prayer can also protect
our loved ones from all kinds of unseen dangers. The posture you choose
can impact your family for generations to come.

Issue Your Decree for Your Family

In Jesus's name:

I decree that as for me and my house we will serve the Lord.

I decree that no weapon formed against my family shall prosper.

Every wicked assignment against this family is cancelled in the name of Jesus.

I decree divine protection and declare that the angels of the Lord encamp about us.

The blood of Jesus is applied to the door post of our home.

I release the power of the resurrection to bring healing, deliverance, and restoration to every member.

I decree that my children are trees of righteousness.

I decree that the power of every generational curse over this family is broken all the way back to Adam. I decree that our blood line is cleansed from sin and iniquity.

I decree that my family will be saved and serve the Lord in holiness and righteousness.

I decree the blessings, success, peace, and the favor of the Lord are over our home.

MY IDENTITY IN CHRIST

"Therefore if any man be in Christ he is a new creature: old things have
passed away; behold all things have become new."

(2 Corinthians 5:17 KJV)

As I look at the last several decades of my life, I cringe to think what
my life would have been like had I not been certain of my identity in
Christ. What I am sharing with you in this book took me years of struggling with shame, insecurities, and anxiety. It is impossible to operate
in our authority as believers if we aren't firmly rooted in our identities.
I believed the bible, and as confident as I thought I was in my faith, I
really struggled with my identity. I wrote out some biblical affirmations
to remind me who the bible said I was through my union with Christ.
Next, I committed to declaring those affirmations daily. At first, they
were rote words spoken without meaning. But eventually, they dropped
from my head into my spirit, and that's where my transformation began.
That transformation can begin for you, too.

Decree Your Identity in Christ

Decree this over your life and get ready for transformation.

In Jesus's name:

I reject every false identity that doesn't align with who God says that I am.

I decree that I am a new creation in Christ.

I am made in the image of God. Old things have passed away and all things have become new.

I decree that I am fearfully, wonderfully, uniquely, and originally made by God to be me.

I am the righteousness of Jesus Christ.

I am part of a royal priesthood. I am redeemed by the blood.

I decree that I am a child of God most high.

I am in union with Christ. I am his joy and delight.

I have been redeemed and purchased by the blood of Jesus Christ. I am a joint heir to the throne. My citizenship has been transferred from the kingdom of darkness to the kingdom of light.

I am fully empowered by God to walk out my destiny.

I am established and secure in who you have called me to be.

I reject and denounce every old stronghold, mindset, lie.

I am created in the very likeness and image of my father God and I am becoming more like him.

I am seated with Christ in Heavenly places far above principalities.

I am unconditionally loved by God. I am accepted and affirmed by my heavenly father.

My father is the creator of the universe and that makes me royalty.

DECREEING MY AUTHORITY

"Behold I give you authority to tread on serpents and scorpions and over all the power of the enemy."

(Luke 10.19 KJV)

Jesus left his disciples with his name and authority to heal the sick, raise the dead, cast out demons, preach the gospel, and legislate and decree on the earth. This power and authority has been given to all believers, but it must be activated and sometimes even enforced.

You are not helpless and powerless to the attacks of the enemy or your life circumstances. It is also worth noting that we can't operate in true authority unless we are under authority. Open your mouth and activate the power to legislate in your realm of jurisdictional authority.

Issue Your Decree of Authority

In Jesus's name Decree:

I decree and declare that according to Luke 10:19, I walk in my authority as a believer. I take up the shield of faith; I wear the breastplate of righteousness; on my feet I am wearing the shoes of peace.

I am walking in authority. I am more than a conqueror through Christ Jesus.

I am seated in heavenly places with Christ Jesus far above principalities and power.

No weapon formed against me shall prosper. I cancel every trick, scheme, and plan of the enemy.

At my decree mountains crumble.

Whatever I bind on earth is also bound in heaven. I thank you God that in all things you cause me to conquer.

Where my feet tread, I take the land. I have authority and power to trample upon serpents and scorpions and over all the power of the enemy.

For though I walk in the flesh, I am not waging war according to the flesh. For the weapons of my warfare are not of the flesh but have divine power to destroy strongholds. I destroy arguments and every lofty opinion raised against the knowledge of God, and I take every thought captive to obey Christ.

I decree that you God teach my fingers to fight and my hands to wage war.

The works of the devil over my life are destroyed.

THE MOUNTAIN OF FEAR

"Fear thou not; for I am with thee: be not dismayed; for I am thy God: I will strengthen thee; yea, I will help thee; yea, I will uphold thee with the right hand of my righteousness."

Isaiah 41:10 (NKJ)

It takes bold faith to move the mountain of fear. Use these decrees as a sling shot to slay the giant of fear in your life and bring it down.

Issue Your Decree to the Mountain of Fear

In Jesus's name:

No weapon of fear formed against me shall prosper.

I choose to walk by faith not by what I see.

I decree that I am as bold as a lion.

I decree that my life is characterized by faith and not fear.

I break the power of all fear, terror, torment, anxiety, worry, and stress operating in my life.

I decree that patterns of fear and anxiety are replaced with faith and perfect peace.

I have perfect peace because my mind is set on you Lord.

I decree that every fiery arrow of fear is now quenched by the shield of faith.

I decree that I walk in power and love; my mind and emotions, sound and stable.

I speak to every mountain of fear threatening my life and I command it to be cast into the sea.

DECLARING VICTORY

**"Now thanks be unto God, which always causeth us
to triumph in Christ, and maketh manifest the savour of his
knowledge by us in every place."
2 Corinthians 2:14 (KJV)**

You were made for victory. However, victory doesn't just happen. It has to be intentional. Victory is a mindset, and it all starts with what you are thinking. When we are born again, we enter into the victory that Christ accomplished on the cross. Yet that victory must be appropriated.

You are not a mere victim of whatever circumstance you find yourself in. God has empowered you to effect change in your territory and realm of influence. Your victory is tied to your authority. Open your mouth and command victory.

Issue Your Decree for Victory

In Jesus's name:

I decree that through the blood of Jesus I have absolute victory.

I decree that I live a life of victory. I am more than a conqueror through him.

God always causes me to triumph. Victory is the only option for me.

My mind is set on victory. I am born to win. Everything that I touch prospers.

Victory is flowing through my veins. I am breathing victory, because the greater one is in me.

Every demonic assignment and attack of the enemy is cancelled against my life.

God will cause the enemies that have risen up against me to fall down before my face. They may come against me one way, but they will flee seven different ways.

Some may trust in horses and chariots, but my trust is in the name of the Lord.

I decree that I am advancing in forward motion. I rebuke every power commissioned to impede my progress.

I decree that I can do all things through Christ; failure is not an option.

I enter into the victory that Christ secured when he overcame the world. I am an overcomer.

SALVATION

"But what saith it? The word is nigh thee, even in thy mouth, and in thy heart: that is, the word of faith, which we preach; That if thou shalt confess with thy mouth the Lord Jesus, and shalt believe in thine heart that God hath raised him from the dead, thou shalt be saved. For with the heart man believeth unto righteousness; and with the mouth confession is made unto salvation."
(Rom.10:8 KJV)

People laughed and talked as the whistle blew and new passengers boarded. The passengers riding in the train would never make it to their intended destination. This train racing at breakneck speed was no ordinary train. The final destination of this train was hell. At any point the passengers were free to get off the train, but they were completely oblivious to the imminent danger.

Where will your final destination take you after this life ends?

Anyone who hasn't received Jesus Christ as their savior, like the people on the train, would be bound for hell. The good news is that God loves us. He sent his son to die for us, to forgive us of our sins, and to give us eternal life. Not only life but a relationship with him. If you are born again, your name is written in the book of life in heaven.

The single most important decision you will ever make is the decision to follow Jesus Christ. The most important decree you can ever utter from your lips is the declaration of your salvation. If you have accepted God's plan of salvation you have legislated a decree. That decree transferred your citizenship from Satan's kingdom of darkness to God's kingdom of light. If you have never accepted Jesus Christ as Lord and savior, why not settle your final destination here and now.

Issue Your Decree of Salvation

If you would like to make Jesus Christ Lord of your life, open your mouth and decree:

Lord as I come to you today, I realize that I am a sinner.

I ask you to please forgive me for my sins.

I confess with my mouth and believe in my heart that Jesus is your son. I believe he died on the cross at Calvary for my sins that I might be forgiven and have eternal life in the kingdom of heaven.

I believe that Jesus rose from the dead. Now I ask Jesus that you come into my life and be my Lord and savior.

I repent of all my sins.

I confess with my mouth that I am born again and cleansed by the blood of Jesus.

From this day forward I will live for you and serve you only.

WRITE YOUR OWN DECREE

"Write ye also for the Jews, as it liketh you, in the
king's name, and seal it with the king's ring: for the writing which is written in the king's name, and sealed with the
king's ring, may no man reverse."

(Esther 8:8 KJV)

Write your own decree.

Decree

Scriptural Basis

STRATEGY

Use this section to write your strategy.

My Goliath

Strategy

Action Plan

Step #1

Step#2

Step#3

ABOUT THE AUTHOR

Sandra Cavallo is an author, minister, speaker, educator, blogger, and entrepreneur.

After years of teaching writing as an English teacher, she decided to release her own voice as an author. She is dedicated to writing books that inspire believers to grow in their faith and relationship with God.

Sandra is also the president and founder of Bride and Dove Ministries International. Bride and Dove is a ministry that empowers women to walk in victory, wholeness, and purpose. Her ministry has been a catalyst for transformation in the lives of women through powerful revelatory teaching, prophetic ministry, supernatural healings, and miracles.

As a mother of four amazing children, Sandra artfully balances family, career, and ministry. When she isn't authoring inspirational books she enjoys gardening, walking, and refurbishing vintage furniture. Learn more about Sandra at www.sandra cavallo author.com, Instagram(@bridendoveministries), or Facebook(@Sandracavallo).

STAY CONNECTED WITH SANDRA

You can chat with Sandra on Facebook@sandracavallo, on Instagram@bridendoveministries, or visit her website at www.sandracavalloauthor.com